Warrant Error

Also by Robert Sheppard

Poetry

Returns
Daylight Robbery
The Flashlight Sonata
Transit Depots/Empty Diaries
(with John Seed [text] and Patricia Farrell [images])
Empty Diaries
The Lores
The Anti-Orpheus: a notebook
Tin Pan Arcadia
Hymns to the God in which My Typewriter Believes
Complete Twentieth Century Blues

Edited

Floating Capital: New Poets from London (with Adrian Clarke)
News for the Ear: A Homage to Roy Fisher (with Peter Robinson)
The Salt Companion to Lee Harwood
The Door of Taldir: Selected Poems of Paul Evans

Criticism

Far Language: Poetics and Linguistically Innovative Poetry 1978–1997
The Poetry of Saying: British Poetry and Its Discontents 1950–2000
Iain Sinclair

Warrant Error

Robert Sheppard

Shearsman Books
Exeter

First published in the United Kingdom in 2009 by
Shearsman Books
58 Velwell Road
Exeter EX4 4LD

http://www.shearsman.com/

ISBN 978-1-84861-018-7

Cover image by Patricia Farrell.

Contents

The War had Ended, it had not Ended

Killing Boxes 8–10

No distant figure cuts diagonals across
the hot war which fleshed this near
scorched field they thrive on threat
citizens perfectly informed of 'trouble
ahead' drift under the flickering syntax
of a virtual journey rolled along
disconnected whorls of mud-ruts
easy arrest made permanent sacrifice
is thrust upon them their own juices
drug them across the defrosting stubble
of last year's crop   No grass
grows through these scattered flints

7 February 2003

Carpets woven with jargon surrender
monkey ground level realism pumps
a Kalashinikov before the gold cupola
a tight wrinkled lip of double-stitch

Every night you fall asleep invaded
by this market target couch drill

an embedded journo pillowed on gas
buys a free full monster with an
empty promise your night vision
goggles catch the first line of his
collateral excised scribble '*barging*

in on targets' struggling with his war
poem the dark god of his sonnets
freeze framed death tools downed

29 March 2003

Self emptive victims shimmy to
the umbrella skeleton weepings
of Mars
            'regret' the ancient
wheeled ordure spilling sewage spice
where they gnaw gnats' gristle
on a rubbished ground plan

Sex down the tar on sparrows before
a dodgy House
                        law games shake
depleted prayers to your stump
the gazelle's eyes have it
clearly somebody's brother's
missing in a ghazal of mass ifs

The direct cost of life is a hit
single radio vomit over reach
over Babel's Tower blowing the
red caps scorches a French
veto
           a horlicks of humans
and freedom fries

27 June 2003

Warrant Error

What better disguise for evil
than sonnets?

Bill Griffiths

September 12

Immensity's blade rushes the wind and
grieves a full deck of bad luck

A managed democracy dances in tune
to a spread-cleft litany, as the Queen's English
warbler, toned to death, unstrews his truth

The blind justice hangs his slogan. Stop.
Burgeon a burden for the chant laureate
entuning and consuming his own genius. The comedy
terrorist brags his mince as roast beef

No peace fries up on a multiple mind grill,
dithering states in desperate times: the sandy
trap-door promise of paradise rusted by frost.
The biggest part of self weakens its softest
option: its cast out old iron alibi song

Steam from the nostrils of the talking engine,
Nervous sweat, stain your place in history.
I myself believe no matter anti-voiced

A crowd's pellicle riddled with restraint as
bulldozers cut deep veins in the sand.
Veiled bodies are piled in, no happy hour for
a last prayer, no compensatory *homaranismo*

I'll buy it, the testimony of the dead, the
imageless human cost: dark stars aloft
and dirty bombs below. I pay with portions
of myself billed in flickering slices. Gifting
the price, a real pain I say: 'As

soon as I write I I am gone (I am not) I
say (to 'my' self): "*Make yourself scarce*

Each creaking oak beam evokes catastrophe
the erotics of raw terror the frisson that
talking will make it happen, acknowledged pain
dispensed at each doorstep. An

index made in just being Britain
invokes threat itself its wincing
nomination held hostage by
shutting our eyes or gnawing
the dry grains of near-certainty

Lips sealed our mouths threaded for
easy snoop and sniper

Our heritage conscience cools the
pre-judgement of history's closure
a hissing that stripes the swart tarmac

Cream light drips
through a moist
sky. Somewhere above the
clouds airliners with
the wrong tickets are

eased out of the
story. Mute pictures

of misery provoke dream
helicopters hovering over
the 'problem', unable to land

Breaking into my
neighbour's house to silence
his burglar alarm I
intervene in history

Whose body crackles with self-quotation, tape-
loop requiem to which it loosens its step?

Your own secret department shuffles your
script, an Unconscious as collective as
responsibility. Or guilt. It's drift. No sifted
evidence while group-think shifts to shafting

Enough! Statutes selve up the sovereign
vote of little appeal, tagging new
lags, to purify the tribunals of the tribe!

Sense a Bright's light relief now an animated chip
of multi-kulti mufti moons across Baghdad as
rapid-eye as a dream of prime-ministerial photo-op:
a fantail of microphones lays his fantastic egg, and
blitzed martyr-bits pile up in paradise, next door

Frost-sharpened sunlight burns
the skin. Between the staves of vapour-
trails a sprinkle of the promised sand sings *I*
met a traveller from a sleeping cell

Capital stampedes its gushing ruts, desires
the eye's friendless fire on flesh in gloom
moving in tune to propulsive gash and gown

The aesthete of barbed-wire corsets plumes
for an incendiary flâneur, blown in premature
invagination. Bodies fill with his self-less throttle,
humming on the radioactive breeze
for phantasmal reward sold as debt

The figure in the doorway is bled away
by policed light that invades the portal

Honour killing slaps a legal face on, when
the evidence takes a life of its own. A breach of
police cooks the entrails warm, holocaust rap

Clawed whip behind a uniformed back:
Switch off your mobile during prayers.
Jihad handcuffs locked into media ecology;
all chatter intercepted @bobmarley123
declares White Meat unprepared for barbecue

They remember women as sperm-capped
mountain ranges, out of range, bespoke

bombers in tailored suicide vests, who cannot
drive their delivery van straight—while MI5 bugs
old lectures on Poussin, trying to break the code!
The fourth world war forgives itself forever

Corseted in his cross-hairs for her caveman pockets,
something goes off in her hand and something
goes very dark. He's a mission to come on her open
territory. She prays upside down as he plays God
away on business, fingering her laptop trigger

Done for a whore's breakfast she loads herself into
his strip-search vest as he sprays his self with love

She's fashioning his new long range out of her wide
world vagina flicked across her dead lover's finger,
slaps on his goggles in the rubble action replay
and spills generation funds on the saintly dust. He

pushes his Big Picture into her head. She blows it
away. Then he rewinds to the comic Big Bang:
blistering flesh bursts like a blown-up condom

Intervene in *err* . . . history impure terror full stop
incognito explodes his own cover at what
he plans to do thinking makes him happen stop
follow the line tightly packed hips sway the crowd

He's a burnt-out *f-f-f*-fuck-box *ah!* you'll waltz
across his set, the CCTV-free short-cut alley stop

His tongue tingles like a *um* fuse then onto
the triad his poisoned tube is pointing stop
fast-forward to where he fear-fucks a corpse

in a transfer-tube marked import stop
read in five or in the sand-pit he plays
with an imaginary *uh* friend *no no* enemy stop
like the 'child he never was' his pit-bull strung
up before the *erm* . . . next war started?

Spiked footsteps, pierced sound,
push love, wheels turning, through his body

His stutter slot trips a new paw-print stage
of psychotic re-enactment, aloft with 9/11
footage on the scorched hooves of history

Heavenly transport hums on dirty wires.
Flecks drip onto his battery fan *Look!* flick
the stale sweat of his pre-emptive terror
breezing a brass tiger across his florid cheeks
(the shifting voice of my thumbnail pause

What am I *err…* for? Echoic *c-c-c*-cave-cell
or self, I splutter anti-matter, the deep *mu-mu-*
mutter of auto-interrogation, self-torture. I am.
Useless to stop anything believe me *leave me*

The shutter-stop tricks a new poor print. Staged,
the evidence takes off a lie of your own, a bleachy
kiss that strips the warts *too much*

A chord and a whip? Behold your deformed back! In
the inflammatory century blown in promissory notes
rabid-eyed in a drama of primed monster photo-ops,
they option the past. Irony's out with an old sunk ally,
tongs of love un-gripped by the sane divorce to sever

Several darts are lighter. They teach restrictions
to heavenly gaudy statesmen. They re-locate
a new sense shelved for their new wharf outing,
the extraordinary City, where they channel hate

calibrate consumption's sub-limits on the caking of a
horlicks, the binding gossip of conscript kickers

no
supreme
court
waves
checks

on
migrants
plotting
whose

brave
facelets

onto
identity
theft

March 10

Burn friendlies on the wreck of human
terror the body of the people O!
Erato! scorched by the blaze of blue-on-blue

Eye witness. *The same railway station.* We.
Search out the others' errant gunshots

Enchanting for democracy O! Muse you wing it
for shepherds sporting iambic lambs on
the platform so enthralled by Love bo-
peeping his fluttery sonnet in Venus' softest target I

miss my earthly transport, and survive. No
golden glove thrusts from the dust. *Erratum*
for Erato: Nobody drops into the same
device twice. Human error. Petrified watch. Our
sponge of blood drips into *the same device forever*

WHO OWNS YOUR FACE? IT FLESHES
ON ALL OUTWARD EYES SIZING YOU

SONNET **X** PULLED OUT BETWEEN THE STOPS,
LABIALS IN THE LABYRINTH: ORPHIC RESONANCE
AROUND THE RINGING TUBE, OR FICKLE ERATO
TICKLING THE LOVESTICK POCKET

REFERENCE TO **X** IS A REFERENCE TO THE SUBJECT
MATTER OF THIS POEM. **X**, TRUE AT THE TIME
OF PUBLISHING, HAS NOT GIVEN PERMISSION. UP.
ESCAPE FROM THIS SMOULDERING FACT. TURN
AGAIN SO IT MIGHT SMILE BACK AND NOT BOIL
          DOWN TO

A POLLUTED POOL OF TABLOID MYTH, OR RISE AS
A PILLAR OF SMITHEREENS SUCKED BY GERMS.
X PLAYS IN YOUR EYES, SMARTING

Every dark is tighter, as each prescriptive
joy is held in check: precipitous release
without charge. Domestic advert for a bidet a long
mirror a civilisation. Just look at yourself

Watch what you're doing a rule with no game
in the front room you're on your back on
your own behind these friendly lines' prosthetic whine.
You empty yourself in a way to make you
you, and catch her foiling stare as you nebulate

Even now you unspeak a tongue
holed up in history's traffic, to assemble
grid-locked love bits at her tightening lips

Sex selving a sonnet for her for making
love is making love is making love is

A collection-source lights up the
heights of post-humanism and queue-
jumps the love-raft in survivalist fury!
Extinction, at whoever's hand, guarantees.
It can deify can worship but can never love

Total death affords the only access. Infidel
conscripts that final day will be spent
to coerce eternity. If paradise
        were to persist without earth

what matter. Ab-
    solute dis-incarnation   redemption refutes

        the one true purity is deletion   a white
sheet   for the lover's face   don't look into
    those eyes   level humanity in your selves

'Shut the Fuck up!' the Ambassadors of
Democracy chorus across blind windscreens.
Weak knees assume that law's single statute

Saddam is the bouquet in their dustbins.
Their heavily guarded statements eulogise
his swimming trunks flapping from a tree,
the colossal wreck of his white Oldsmobile

*

'He could be fun! He knew some verses
about the loved and un-level sands

how God might permit him to turn America
into a shadow of itself. He borrowed men
with borrowed guns to chant his
homemade poem: "To her Doom she sails,
clothed in Great Illusion   *too close to home*

impossible to tell this story how it
ends every word recounts the eye
witness zipped lips beside My
Self bitter non-identical restless lyric

shifts the guilty at their bench
unable to sit unable to stand won't pass

or pass over into a *st-st-st-*
utter swallows the whole one figure **X**
replaces every other
other the dust
breath pure coincident mutter embodies

dream as dead sleep the path of Ab-
negation cluttered with tongues telling you
like   it is   writing

Dissensus-uncensored citizens their post-fluidarity
Jams the geodesic sepulchres of GCHQ

The ballet of chatter threatens the iron triangle
A-theism in-corporates the earth's blown powder
But resistance to existential terror within
Microquakes at neo-feudal controls
Quivers flesh *contra* the Universal Event

Military ground aches with mediatized Odes
While secular *fatwas* begin the law of rules
Territorialized apostrophes in the dead mouths of victors

We are in love with Eros and you with a suitcase
Dirty device crafted by cells O! new
Selves unresolved on a new war footing
Self-made utopias   draped in black

He breaks off to listen to the
news. Standing at the top
of the stairs he catches
the muffled litanies of *because*
we can because . . . Eros-

ion of other people's liberties
he is coerced to give up. He's
given up himself a unilateral

suspension of sovereign operations.
In his refrain of terror 'we' is more than
twice his love story. In most respects
he's an ordinary citizen. He cannot wait

for his promised ID card to stamp out who
he is, twinkles stolen from his lustrous eyes

Watch how they leave their scream-shot
meat in global entunement
to ID-spasms, pushing their a-
symmetric war chants, these Poets

followed by the Errant. They spew
narcissistic compassion for the As-Yet
-Invisible-Event, without purchase. They

celebrate redemptive sublimity in the shaking of
captive beards raked with bristling electrodes . . . .

My other's Other is my enemy, forcing
twitters of war within skin-selves. Organs
without bodies crack bone codes, take
on the shades of Immortal Animals. The a-
theistic body screws its tools down to earth

Self-othering hood Klans one's unbecoming
the obsolete body art of choreographed excess
a video diary that couldn't care more or less

Floating on flesh-hooks in betweenness aloft
who licks the blinding gusset of combat knickers

kicks a pile of fleshly rags shovelled by rubber-
necking rednecks? Instead of thumbprints
they press sweat-stains into the dustiest corners.
A body regime splintered by such loving
inhabits what it shall never possess

A barbed obscenity haunts for an extra ear
the parasitic cyborg whose hearts and minds
surrender to the body's self-absorption.
Under the hood maggots nest like emotion

Eros
rose reso-

lved made love unselved into lover or l-
oser, whom-
so'er Erato emboldened head to head with death.
Accelerated amnesia in the face of hysteric
obsession. Suspended sentence in favour

of pre-cautionary ends. That secretly invites Doom
as the terminal Event that will make it make
sense you know it makes sense. Sensing
a nuisance fact unfolds historic succession . . .

'There will be no more
security reports
for security reasons

Through slatted blinds you spy another
writing a stuttery scrawl of spidery infringement.
You chisel each other into pedestal fear,
nailed to combat mottoes, slashed
and slotted in your mirror-script encryption

You're unknown unknowns, improper nouns
once announced in a Cold War Nuke Ode.
Same-selved you live: dead meat on the other's
plate garnished with knowns, lashed to the past

Sirens sing at the fringes of your passage.
Sleep plunders the sickly green of paramedics
under shutters. *History was yesterday*

In the live moment splintering between two deaths
invade this single body and unblade the truth

December 2003–May 2004

Smoking Gun

Invisible Epaulets

She stares through mascara
repulses of pure thought, her navel

long departed to synthetic heaven,
blanked-out windows in shady suburbs.
She is the muse of our age,

a jigging bunch of unturning keys to
all we hold dear, when all we hold
they turn back on us in defiant dubiety.
Their faith is all dancing, some

peasant pikes. Our hero is sacrificed,
his patrician javelin reforms into
a cry of joy retuned to a howl, and
victory is recast as victimhood
to deface the human covenant

Saved or Saved for Later

One thought in up-spiralling motes disperses
speculation, the long decipherment
of blind perception into mute neuter sense

For a glove of melting digits swap a slow
swallowing of flesh by sable noon. All explanations
are theological, no doubt, waged in a market
of bad form. You wrap the world about you

as a mantle of extraordinary experience
but your knees give way to oncoming celebrity.
Guilt chokes like cheap perfume rising off the
runway. You record delivery of the miracle,
weighed down by divine possession

What happens during the re-enactment
may be more complex than a life of its own

A Bit Rich

Hardly passing for an event at all, it reflects
the day's rush and the glint of your irises.
Your frog-eyed goggles track our stabs
on the chalk-line, sold to the enemy

The pointed show of your black shoe points
to where the inexplicable explanations lie
curled at the heart of black stone, pulling faces
the hard way between tufts of sky grass
and spoon. Waggle your wings like a tart!

embarrassed by our brittle celibacy, embraced
by your little celebrity! Below, the Earth rolls

from wingtip to wingtip, flecked with targets
rumbling through the Bramleys, as salmon
buck up stream through lemon-juiced runs

Lip Synch

Microphones prod the crystal air he sips
His jacket drapes his firm shoulder
The warrants are safe in his back pocket
Spotlights behind cast no-business shadows
Their poisoned harmonies take no prisoners

One of his nipples winks like a warlock's third eye
It's a node of soul-meat a lizardy pinhead

A sugary outcrop settles on the earth's crust
A black diagonal scars its sheet of snow
Everything surrenders to gravity's swoon, he mimes

He smiles a snapshot bleached of himself
Unrepresentative representatives
Are ranked behind his declining machine
Their helmets are unhappy misfits like them

The Audience at All Costs

She's a pin-up in a factory of eunuchs
dampened by their own enthusiasm

He's deep in communion with egg-yoke
bursting on his silk neck-tie, lawn
handkerchief mopping, the disconsolate
consul fashioned by the wrong sloped moustache

He pushes and pulls the tune she
squeezes and stretches to smithereens.
Her nice legs work the plugged-up crowd

She flees like a love-lorn heroine
from her repertoire: the slow punctuation
of cutlery grating against a plate. The dying
drop their eyes, not on life, but on
death. She is the jargon made flesh

Mooring Song

Dawnlight streaks
the ice-capped peaks
Guitars sleep
on their backs and snore

Her tongue whips
through her mask it
Seeks a sucking mirror its flick

—

Ering advances the puckered O *his*
tongue shoots
He dresses for the ride
drifts near a reef
Of cuffs as they sing

our skeleton remains
Fleshed in one voice

Black Flower

You are neither inside the room nor outside. You melt
in piny breeze from unlatched windows catching
shadows, a hint of coffee from the cafetière

Consultant to this enterprise, you de-contract from history,
decapitated consciousness: the eyes the ears
the brain collecting fitful data still from the world
as it's lost. The fateful apologia of the mob fades.
Azure is pure message behind choking smoke

Heads bow over the human mess they've made.
The poet leads the service of remembrance

Within minutes they've forgotten. Nothing. The prince
waggles his ears as corpses are pulled out of nowhere.
Personality teeth gleam from his chattering person
his coiffure set atremble like a tea-party jelly

That Public Feeling

Matter becomes consciousness once more
a botched Botticelli the face crushed
its propositional perspective withered and black
as a dead man's hand, rises
from the waves on cue

The face crushed from bubbling light
her translucent bikini adverts a voice

Her hair tossed high and fractal
she's a broken Barbie bobbing up
your private beach dodging
the landmines and the barbed wire singing

A freak voice unspeakably human
breaks the wavelength of our audition
fools anonymity with the terror it flashes

Giving Up Whatever Ghost

He slouches in the front row of the stalls
adjusting opera glasses at the bridge of his nose,
inspects the safety curtain. You scrutinise his nape,
scrubbed, beneath his slicked-back denial of hair

The curtain rises; his glasses descend. Democracy
breaks out, caught in its own crossfire:

Teargas bursts the centre of the crowd; it fans out
cursing and gasping. One hand reaches
for the bread; three mouths moisten at this

The soprano's dress slips down her frame.
The ringlets of her wiry wig cascade, shake
as crescendo beckons; her throat tightens.
Her shoulders struggle free into perfect air
of purest song; they embrace wordless blackout

Ruffling My Feathers

One breast bobs free chilled with gooseflesh
in the bitter wind. A cold snap at her fringed

snatch. She's trying to get me to repeat
her mouth-sounds fluting years of her
need to be loved into trilled breath syllables

Concentrating hard decoys her younger self.
She can't sell this one to the workers! She's
spread against the wall in coy thumb-sucking.
Her hymen breaks with sheer attention to detail;
unsupported stockings wrinkle at her knees

She bears a pale ghost tag on her skin.
My eyes brim dark pools to drown her celestial light,
her fresh mascara, her sharp lipstick, to flood
the echoing hollow of her shaved armpit

Without Issue

Black triangle masked face lifts her beyond
personhood. There is back story to sell, but no coin
for her slot: *Spots of blood stained the pool*

At first they were bobbing fruit in soup
then they acquired faces then thrashing
limbs they became human. They achieved
voice, munching the melody with bared teeth
bad taste. The stench of species solidarity

Tramlines trench the wet road shunting
steamy boxes packed with silence uncertain
which language to unwrap. Overhead wires
pull the city together tilted from horizontals

Jack-in-a-Box chatterer jumps back seat leather
slit (her navel winks like tomorrow's bullet hole

Macro News

Woman split as thought in a mirror
Just a hint where the skirting board
Shifts abutted the way she drops her
Splitting work bag the same thing twiced
Folds behind her back in handcuffs condemned

The top of the dock slices across
Her neck the bewildering mechanics of justice
The yawning jury guilty as sin steals
Glassy glances and ravenous gulps of gin

Her claw locked on a compliant shoulder
Now one toe taps at the verdict

Her hair's adjustable wave could be the
Point of her careless existence our cleansing
As an art forms around her neck

Sturdy Bipods

The Wolf's porky sister unpeels potatoes,
crouched under severe staring calendars.
Reciting exhaust she could take your weight

Sexual transgression could take them all
She could nibble the family to bits

Dripping the pack of air as they vanish
with lard she softens the weft of the carpet.
At night her eyelids fall over bulging rubber.
Light the blue touch snout with a gusset

He sucks his pipe, elbows on knees.
His is a private part played out in public;
he's playing the identity card, funnelling
himself into the boot of the nineteen-fifties,
fly-leg stubble across his chinny-chin-chin

Over the Balcony

She declares the redundant square,
Old hat, handbag and hanky:

Bones rattle above machine gunning
Antics to belittle us all, a long
Black evening revolt. Debris
Bridges her driven fingers home

Pours between towers, dumps wreaths of grain
In sand-winnowed alleyways. She might be
The leaf sheltering our choice, or the teeth of all luxury
Which has not been divined,
To release our first cluster, the subject of history

Gnashing crusader the way she catches the light
She says:
The terrorists' aircraft blows its own nose

Like I'm Nowhere

When I grow up I'll become the next day's
lesson from the Human Dog!
I'm praying, my hands pressed together
in bullet-sprayed breeze! I live in a darkening time!

I don't know which ear controls what!
(Exclamation marks can stand on their heads.)
Your smile tears your faces to pieces;
it coaxes me to speak to the muse, as
men in macks tick their bikes across the line

In the misted signal box they crank and crash,
and barriers rise. We're becalmed
among deafening billows. Guess whose name

fills the corporate cage? I guess I'll leap free now
into temporality's instant collapse

. . . there has been a rip

in reality, a fissure, a sort of plaster
over her private parts, a kidnapper's
masking-tape gag. A patch
of prohibition. Whatever she does she
cannot bring herself off, condemned

to a purgatory of porn where oily
lovers worship each other's tools. Her itchy
fingers ache for a sticky love-muscle

to spasm. Tight-arsed Rückenfigur
before the ice-capped peaks

of his ambition, paralysis
and yearning balance 'like frogs
on a log'. *This is my claw;*
it is chained to my other hand...

Spasm or Whiz

Funk! he'd yelled the night before
I just want funk! funk! funk! the fifth
point of the compass the erupting cabin boy!

his polished love-muscle on a park bench
oily for a soft scientist. Crashed
in the 'brace-brace' position, he was the sole
survivor of the party, cowled in his lamé jacket

Waking up his threads in the morning
the bag-faced boy zips up his shorts

Enblossoming the ledge a mossy merkin,
the window-frame's suspended PVC
fishnet. Between our nowheres
the clownish check shirt checks out his person.
But peel open people and people fall out

The Shot

To get the shot? Difficult, because the man's head
is bowed, as if in acknowledgement of guilt.
The offence was capital; the law is crooked.
White knuckles squeeze the wire

Blackout absorbs him inch-by-inch so that mask
and erasure rule out unruly flesh and members

This could be animation incarnate or simply
the effigy shaking from the human covenant.
Handheld recorders float as a pummelling fist
punctuates each verb; recorded space,
grey noise. The vein above his ear winks. Later,

a woman enters, shrugs, loosens her dress,
unzips it at the back. If this were life there could be
love, Stygian soup, abstract and concrete swans

Given Up the Host

The ventriloquist with the wooden smile thinks
that the bruise's owner owns the embrace:

The divorcees sit shoulder to padded shoulder
in each other's body heat, released after several
lifetimes as hostages. Her uncle's feud
with the hereditary bandit king is 'resolved'.
She shrinks back into the umbra of her armpits

His shades anonymise him. His op-art tie tags him,
conjures his illusion of post-modernity,
marionettes him towards her squeaky decree

This is a game without a theory. Your eyes
are muddy stones, your nostrils bolt-holes in stubble.
You're perfect! Your tongue is a moist waggle-poke
catching the light, or gathering shadows

Heritage Trial

Like Orpheus, she looks back.
                                        With
spider fingers she pokes stolen fruit
into her leery mouth. The bloated leeches
of her blood lips curl. She melts
under her own hair, stick-on melancholia

Trailing across the valley wall, a chain of soot
from the burning village. Blanched on the brink,
the blank-faced castle faces the day

Something washes the day away. It won't
flow together as collective memory. I'll
be forced to release a minority report *Of Things*
Quotidian—but Parliament is suspended

A pointed beard furrows a path to calamity.
Veneration recommences in the morning at nine

Berlin Inventive

Up the back alley of Karl-Marx-Allee
a custom-built prospectus of unreal estate
the proletarian stickman pisses away Luisenbrau
supplicants tremble for a Chinese blowjob

A tendrillous dandelion sprouts from his penis
a tense blending of muscle and will
we puff-fluff spoors onto the icy breeze

Bathing ourselves in the Spartan chill
shatters the reflection of our dipping limbs

When I wake I'm stateless. On the
chalk-board an up-date of the head-count
purged sheets and pulsing matter
no tungsten pellicle slips over my eyeballs
I can't overstate the state I'm in

Parisian Download

Who flicks up that alley if you stray from the blvd?
He keeps it light and they shake at his jokes.
He is done, done in. They are done for

His curls curl at the latest terrorist download:
the hacking of the Christian chicken-neck

You've walked through the wrong door (again)
to catch this lot! He tells them stories about
themselves, choked in their choking chokers.
In the grip that grips him, loose skin shaking,
thin ribs wheezing, hands aloft, he recites:

This is what le philosophe *saw last: his Being*
spread like butter across the roof of a Citroën
parked squarely below in its yellow box, a scooter
chained to shutters, and a dwarf juggling hour-glasses

A Nose

A nose-diving orgy of American mettle,
old planes piled high like Iraqi prisoners

slithering their loaded bellies on each other's backs,
falling through fisted coral fighting the sky
of their scrapyard making, erupted
from ocean foam, dispersed into fleece clouds:
a plumber's botched job with cheap sealant

*

A nose spites a face, mouth spits this protest
against anything we want it to be against.
We run with our beating eyes shut
along the dry track's beat to the scrapyard,

the Hollywood pow-wow. Shunning
celebrity we deny the existence of our ears,
the rattling quiverful of quivering arrows

Smoking Gun

At the end of the world you are driven away
in the back of the National Limousine, flashing
your legs that wrapped around the international
affair, past flashbulbs of the Final Edition.
You're looking at skinny girls in the magazine

They are sort of you. They kneel in shorts
on a bed as long and thin as your thumb,
tilted muse of cubist accidentals. Raise
your fist to the smoked-out sky, espy the fringe

of the kerb where shadows chase one another,
the low light giving edge to their pursuit.
Mr Bin Laden is not at home. Not emerging

from his cockpit, not rubbing his good eye.
It's not that beard of white smoke again

April–July 2006

Ordinary Renditions

Liverpool
January–December 2006

I no longer turn up for my own recordings.
I simply send along my voice instead

I walk like half a man with rickets,
a flâneur who talks himself into a blind corner
and is pulped by Situationist thugs

I sleep with my eyes open, spy every
ruck and tuck of the bedroom curtain.
I pull my own plug as I feel my rush,
a bonus heartbeat in the vinyl spiral.

I tell my own story, sing myself to death,
an antique pleasure that slips from its sleeve.
I enter this place with repeatable behaviours.
I get smaller and smaller to everyone else.
I'll not learn to wait in my own bated breath

Look out over the Moses bullrush marsh
and the duck lake that wasn't there, to the dumb
building that still isn't, humming no tune

Identify a green square. Name the soft sands.
Describe the Death Row Groupie,
the gnarled bone on her abandoned plate like a
stripped penis, flakes of flesh along its length

She recites her erotic dead sonnets, bosom heaving,
low gasps. She's a label-eater all right, with
munching taxonomies and a cushioning bar-stool.
On the TV above, the primate of intelligent design
looks as though he's been designed by dumb-bells

But don't look too close—both
his powdered ears are on upside down

‘She skirts the shuttered *Estate Agency*—
blown cover of Bin Laden’s rendered moneyman—
this skinny scally-girl in Persil-white. Trainers
well apart, without comment, without shame, she

gushes piss between them; and lopes off. You perform
your own forming, a blob of porky-pies, wheezing on
about your piggy skin weeping urea, bursting
into pain like a gospel singer screaming
the walls down, as melted cheese flakes from your

gaping cake-hole, shoulders haunched before
widescreen TV, staging its ordinary renditions

Defrost this block of torpor I’m trapped within!
The first law of unintended consequences
re-writes my poem on the final proofs’

Look out of the window in the next poem I'm
writing and remark whatever I put there.
I'll build a —— , then cross it out, or place you
at suppositional locations, littering the littoral,
measuring the sky, body and sea interjacent . . .

Sudden sleet. Blanched haze furs the belly of
blanket cloud. The lake pitted, wind-feathered

Beneath the bobbling pistons of her behind, her spiked
right heel hits the flagstones at an angle, could
buckle her ankle, but it just holds, and lifts

The sun shows out to steam the flags. The grey
slides off to make love in its default position.
It leaves the dry analecta you collect like flotsam:
'Even corruption amongst the moths is poetic'

Arctic wind shoulders me back. Flurries
of imaginary snow fritter away the lake

Ducks fluster on invisible banks, soft lapping
in the fractured darkness which demands
more space than bodies can extend into.
This rush of writing spotlights the present

word only, a smelted ingot of contraband fact.
I must not forget this amnesiac wordster, as he
'sketches' the 'process' between 'agents' and 'units'

How much is that author in the window, the one with
the easy life? Words like 'negotiation' enflame him,
though counting is his guttering release. It's easier
to recount his life than my own, easiest for him to retort:
'Don't drink the water in the ditch where you're dropped'

Black night stiffens the resolve of the window.
Wipe-out rain, a bad sound effect of rain, white-
noises your voices out, rustles up a simpler sound
of God's brass neck talking through His hat

Your ruffled reflection raises the ethical question
as you paste words like 'author' and 'authority'
on the board beyond this screen of your becoming

Wind, though outside, sheers your breath away.
On a traffic island in Hardman St., a kneeler torches the night
in Guantánamo orange, grizzled by a protestant cloud.
Police rush on in yellow. Fleshing blue lights on cars
parked as barriers breed darkness in the dark

Smack a lip or two, ruddied up, roughed up for a smile.
Tonight, Condoleezza Rice is being entertained

The foreign secretary, spotting bare-headed top brass,
swipes the tin hat from his head as he follows
down the steps to Iraq's soft tarmac the secretary of state's
 smile

that's clammed to her face like a category mistake
that dropped down one floor in the lift and emerged
a changeling into the roar of a canvas wind.
Celebrity murderess heads off to a fresh beheading.
Elegant heels lift slender ankles, where he follows

Yawning policewomen guard the spaces in Liverpool
she leaves, a line of orange cones elisions in her diary

Her brain barks orders like a sea captain during desertion.
Abu Ghraib grey ocean lips sharp-toothed cliffs brushed by sun.
The mutineers have taken the dormitory.
As their voices fall asleep, they murmur against her

The stars are inside this afternoon, cloudlessly
turning around our human pivot, a fashion statement
of sorts but its proposition is false. Somewhere
from beyond the constellations comes the voice, the
inevitable human voice, of the non-human

Trace documentary over the filched, the filtered,
the tracks of elsewhither across familiar terrain:

The Asian restaurant drooped in the flag of St George;
the Irish bar shrinking from the kerb of London Road;
the pub opposite promising 'patriotic goings-on';
while shadowy people lope along the lakeside path

The universe dreams itself apart until you recover
the threads, and guide them back into shape: tea-stains
on the cracked white paintwork of our window sill

He speaks well for a man with three heads!
One consists of convoluted meat, all hubris,
atavism and dilucidation. The second is filled
with echoic spaces, you know, Ikea boxes,

enough room for a deodorised ghost. The third
is stuffed full of positive things that make you

self-actualise and grin. In the Book of his Life
we read that he never loved you. Liver-spotted hand
grips the censor's pencil, grey templed pressure-point

Two tables away legs shift like a stale seduction.
The baby's stubby fingers fumble an adult digit;
they splay, distracted, not yet focussed on the
human covenant. At some point he spotted
this page in proof, and marked the error for later

Big rain lips over last century's shallow gutters
and crashes on tonight's last-supperism

Drops leap like pebbles on the puddles
pulsing in winking rings. Two horses
side-by-side, shiver, stamp hooves, buck,

each turning, tuned, to the other's twitch;
its damp breath. The thin man
in the white suit loves the black
woman in the fat dress. They rush out
to catch the crimson sunset together . . .

The shocking pink top on the flame-haired girl
cuts an arc of silk that frames her crystal navel.
Let's christen this our Anti-Star. It'll wink forever
at each trembling embrace we shall put there

As the jongleurs enter, the world becomes a book:
The Boss announces that our strike is over and
we trust him. We return to our chilled kilns

We mould fresh effigies of his children's education.
The rattling of blinds in the breeze rattles, blind.
The lakeside path is carpeted with crushed cartons,
the work of starlings dragging and dropping by the bins,
huddled clumps of shivering silvered feathers

He fought in You-Know-Where. He never speaks of it,
though shrapnel blasts below the trauma-radar;
the anality of evil hoards itself in a pit, spiteful
and pitiless, a death-mark on a birth-mask

They trussed him; 'I'm thinking genocide! Do it!'
His mask-muffled echo is kicked down the toilet

The horizon dead ahead, the aery sheet
of aquamarine hanging from it,
the sharp slope you trip down to the heart
of the whitewashed town, its warnings in Welsh,
the curled lip of the seashore, you have forgotten

. . . like the railway criss-crossing the border, except
it's like voices proclaiming our insect origins
before you're aroused to its resolving noise,
the man who could remember reading solid ink

Something here, immune to the laburnum's ripped sting,
is reduced to its own skeleton, buried in wind-borne grit

The dead thrush, a wet bedraggle, barely registers.
When it resurrects on the slope, it's something with linkage
if only with itself: a gritty photocopy of summer's sudden
            sheets

On the anniversary of the bomb outrage, you don't shout
'I survived!' as you surface from the Tube. You experiment
with high notes, placing them in every piece you play

to remind yourself that you may squeal well above
the capacity of your tubes, well-sustained

Heat burns at the fringes of your reason, strips
flesh off each fresh fingering. You could travel
to the next galaxy fuelled by your presumption,
funded by a fellowship of the ears. Lipless jaws

tap teeth, sockets turn to earthly delights.
Everything in the poem turns spectral, even the
decorative holes in the fabric of our breathing,
or the one word we need, engraved on clear glass,
blasted by harsh sunlight onto the wall beyond

An organism upon the surface of its planet,
contemplating long his depth in creation

even to a solar guttering, or choked charcoal
upon a barbeque, the joined up star-gazer
propped up on elbows, sucks a tube of lager.
Only after the breeze cools under clear dark sky

does walking seem possible, or talk. He
spent the whole day. He watched his ceiling,
the little cracks that spread, the creaks
that presage downpour, dust: a scuff of hot fur
resentful of each invasive impulse . . .

Place them in the sarcophagus, in the space craft—
these five fish mummified in the shape of one big fish—
for the cat, its interstellar journey to the Beautiful West

for Patricia

We slide the week ahead, pause it trembling
at a future instant, somewhere in extensive
time that underwrites each moment.
All our actions are staged on this surface

We'll rest upon it during this event, as he
makes a world, augmenting his resentments.
The person who is absent will constitute his day,
a series of evasions to bind him to all he'll miss.
Everything will curl around the nothing of it

It's a new game, somehow like faulty traffic lights
guarding a hole in the road, blinking like an idiot.
But the sunflower now you place for me in sunlight

is staged on the other side of sense, making love
happen, firing me with its fiery compound eye

I steal myself into the flow of the writing,
tilting diagonals against rectilinear plots.
Rain slants, scored across the sheet. My
umbrella becomes a stop-off for soaked girls,
flattened perfume, stinks off wet pelts

Misread the trickle of blood, iridescent, on a cheek,
a scarlet scar, as dark cherry buttons congeal
on the floor, and the matted skull is squeezed safe

Once inside, I can change this anew: it's piped
in the bistro, selling itself on the jukebox, the voice

of the 'genius' that grates like a food-mixer,
slowly rising to the whining of a drill; or
it's the Arab peeling away to the hostel with shopping.
His alien mobile pop showers him with home

Glandulous green waters, thick on the lake,
Where the Jesus Bird stands on its surface—
Whatever you need to further your identity . . .

The man misrecognises you, shakes your hand,
While you stabilise the fiction that sustains,
Or you'd clatter to the floor like castanets,
Your strings cut by insurgents

From the hold of the Hercules
fourteen coffins are carried
To the tune of Nimrod to the
hushed grief of the hearses

The Mersey ignores these protocols: sandy clouds,
Eddies and swirls, twirl seaweed amid debris, churning;
Like the Vltava we saw in flood: weather vanes
And wine bottles tumbling over and over
On a mad dance running the length of Europe

The lake fashions a gelatinous skin through which
the happy dog plunges into emerald germ-clouds.
Tongues, loose, pulse against the membrane;
a safari suit tangles in a polylingual jungle

She clops by in her new high heels, now
she's discovered the joy of walking taller

You at least work *that* stagger in, the stutter,
the stumble through to a throaty drain
with too much to say—and her bloody kisser.
Jokes in TB's 'farewell' speech are slo-mo mimes
of sea-captains saluting from the bridges of listing

ships in old British films: *our* clipped voices,
their clicking heels. Around the hall, lips curl around
sandwiches—only the cellophane whispers dissent

Is there no single word to hold the hazed
shadow of a person projected through mist?

*

Her tiny knotted filigree—he moistens it.
She shudders from burning ears to curling toes.
The moment it splits her, he stirs. ‘I love a woman
whose lingerie is the same colour as her hat!’

A fact with no flesh on its bone

*

Asylum seekers saunter in a row across the path

The sole woman laughs into her mobile phone

(‘Read my lips!’ purrs the hijab porn-star)

*

Excavations below the misted path to the lake
subtract the ground to leave a tray of sifted earth
the space that once imagined a terracotta army
now flashes tracks of pleasure through your bones

Sparky the Iraqi drops to his knees, slaps his palms
in the pooled blood of the freshly slaughtered.
It is wedding day, and we bear gifts
to the party. Passengers scatter
from the windows burrow into bus seats

Black smoke blossoms above the burnt-out frame,
the skeleton of democracy enveloped in its cloak.
The sun cuts and runs behind dimming imperial marble

An affirmative thumb grinds the old man's eyeball,
feeling the crack and leak of its egg; a swift boot
kick-starts the chorus of 'groaners',
bagged like chickens, cut and dried

But the child chilled on the mortuary slab
bears my name on its blackened toe

Caught beneath both wipers,
clinging to the windscreen,
clutches of brittle leaves
that the winds have driven home

Before he's dumped in the bin,
Saddam beats its lid, as fireworks freak;
frigid crimson on the cusp of dusk

Wild roses, mad with warming, blossom
in a springtime of their own sensing

It's Rumsfeld's last 'certain certainty'.
The black cat and its blackest shadow,
thrown by low sun across the carpet, pad by.
I smile to think bits of myself
scattered about the room

Not just that all objects are lashed by the light of the mind but
    that all
of the objects seem lit by the flash of each other an inter-
    illumined world
blinding glare off the wet flagstones and all kinds of kink to
    stop him

identifying with her testimony she sways tenderly on the
    uneven flags in calf-
hugging high-heel boots the shadow of his head cast (low sun)
    on her back

she turns as if to confront the imprint of his fantasy to conflate
    many a gender
and split open his body or the bodies of those others she may
    be driven to love
words bound on from the wings to synchronise their lips a
    pleasure domain
of willed sighs stealing lipstick kisses drinking each other dry
    her red-seamed
stockings wrinkled for chiming (Toussaint stops to tap the
    New York streetlamp

darting in gusts brilliant gulls hold a fractured formation long
    enough to
drop to the chopped surface of the lake high in bare trees
    white leaves or
plastic bags stark against the bluster he decides to put the
    whole thing in
pushing its brimming shallows almost to the point of spillage
    then pulling.

His breath takes her beauty away, deep
in his body where language measures the world

One breath it takes to be no longer winning a war.
They cup warm palms over each other's cold knees.
Wind shoulders against the flanks of their house;
windows shiver.
They stand in front of it to stand for themselves

It chimes into rhythm that celebrates itself,
this looking at tomorrow, guiding the eye back
to the time of their looking, a swoon into cracks
between history and memory. She dressed in black

from frisking ponytail to stabbing boot toe. Out-
stretching her impossible heels, he buries himself,
moulding her sighs, in soft mammalian heat

A turn in the tide-patterns turns them up, once only,
after 6000 years, these footprints we misread in the sand:
a woman's deliberate step, her child's capering dance,
until the next tide brushes them away. Reversing
the polarities of a phrase short-circuits the sentence

Under dove-grey skies, dark winter coats resolve into form
two warm smiles. Cheered, re-born into consciousness,
we share the watery patches in the grass, the boggy
dip to the blank lake—then part, chilled. Cars plume

sculpted waves as they push through flooding.
The words in the sentence are like stones laid
deliberate in a row, flush or imbricated

The blushing walls of Haditha overlook the human
covenant: We nestle into one another's beastly warmth

November–December 2006

Warrant Error

I Off the Books

A tall man came to their door an
Instance of polite rendition

She was in a loose dressing gown he
Could see a strap it was
The wrong hotel between the killings

Kaleidoscope reassembled history
Moved 'inevitably' towards
Warrantless wiretaps and zap the road
To Damascus was shelled every day

He stuck his fingers in a bag of salt
Zawahiri had them shot filmed it
Following a script
Provided by their enemies they dropped
Leaflets on fields of perfumed martyred corpses

Self-protection was self-consumption scared
Or sacred it's eased into the holiest story
A sonnetized account with the biggest screen test

Local colour was masked by raw
Overheads and the heresy was mere hearsay
When evidently witless their mouths agape they rose
At bungled bugle-blasts jamming Agape and Eros

In the ballad of the blade she bites him
Obliged attack he shoots mightily back in
Terror or error she tries to send the message
From compassion back to passion
She writes releases for rouged regimes

When she's finished she pulls the plug
And he spills the viscous liquid for her

Lots of policemen ran to their door the spies
Who didn't come in from the hot-tub wore
Rucksacks as something foaming fell to the floor
Chemicals chapati flour and shrapnel

She rose from the bed adjusted her tactics
She was candid about her emotions the ones
She had and the ones
She didn't this peroxide was used in my bleach
She said there can be no freebies or friendlies

The city huddled the neighbours close
Pity is a sentiment I hugged to myself

The purpose of shrapnel was to increase
Fragmentation and rapid reaction with a gob on it
He sensed they held the toothpaste in common

There was another town within adjusted cause
Let us reword the world around it so
What the ‘groom’ couldn’t name his fiancée
He was born Trevor Something in Hackney
We squeezed in bombing time before Ramadan

I saw a house fly up in the air it was good
To tickle in that nice little liberal enclave

They’re only up for stripping paint ahem
If I sit here I will commit sins
Cars furred with frost purred round the corner

Mohammed turned so his rucksack was facing
A mother and her child he was amazed he
Couldn’t believe it he was still there
Mute intervention in good old new moon Europe

They scoured the news and erased the story
The liar the witness and the lawyer

The hand that mocked us scarred
Or scared soured the newscasts
Their oblique attacks now roar overhead
The naives are restless during the rapid raids

Compassion is one of the passions
After a regular
Tory system of lower tax nothing beside remains

Species solidarity and its dispersal
In this borrowed shell function as love but
This is the real thing as she
Bends towards him
Not to be unworthy of what happens to them both

Pity spouts spectral behind the mask we're all
Variations on the great unknowable theme she says
Natality is the eruption of politics once
Beyond the jamming you're a ragged fist of flesh

Lustful lustrations pour half-cups for her
Spilling boundless and bare the vernal
Promise of her bucking legs under his tensing arm

This unfurls a light tickling a slight
Feathery ethos while neural
And neutral in local greyscale our leaders
Leak their large-scale verbal promises and
Roar *O bleak attack of global colour*

She transcends mess and message ogles her own raw
Presence and says *some guys just disappeared off the books*

2 English Poems

Rainshine shivers on dull platforms
Phone masts silvered in the gloom like shrines gather the chatter
Of the nation in bunches as elderflower tap the breeze

A single oak is fenced in but broken fences
Stitch landscape into the neat motley of Capital
We glide through sward smeared with mustard
Under clouds like smoke from dead fires centuries old
Rainbow umbrellas flip between the cars and the parishless
        church

Slap-bang in the middle of the country fresh timbers
Naked girders gnaw the ring road of the blue city

The dark girl with long lashes lifts a restless leg to her seat
She reads a biography of our next prime minister
As a tunnel sucks us dry into our own echoes
How English can you get? More so

You ride on a bus called Peter Kropotkin
Past shops with names like Quaff and Klodhoppers
This is not the dream but lines of the poem
That carry your dream in which
A nightmare Neo-Con indites you alone

You are the unclean skin from the fertiliser plot
You'd blow up all those slags dancing around

You are the gas fitter who plans mass murder
You cannot even spell al-Qaida
He deploys smart certainties against
You asleep he invades your interior hunger

You listen to the charges against your name
Quick guilt ignites
Beneath the soft armour of your rising denials

Arrested when the first door was hit
I didn't know what conspiracy meant
Police came in
Like a movie wow this is happening

You get that negative thing that things'll go sour
Prison is another life we're not aware of

I went to the dock in my own bubble guilty
I didn't hear it guilty not guilty
I believed in myself for things to go right

Walls they leave you like boarding school
A table made of cardboard I broke it
I just looked up and said where the hell am I
I'm just human still proud to be British—
I *had my student loan and* he *was doing building*

Belief is sunlight cast down the sheer cut
Taking shadows as hints from the post-industrial summit

Blood-red buffer—history's after-image
Rusts progressively beyond use beyond exchange
We catch a flash of eternal night under the brick bridge

The promised city winks like an ice sculpture
Chiselled by continental trams as cranes
Claw at the remnants of Friday afternoon
Silver execs print shirtsleeves on car windows
They call this the power to think the unconditional

One new building is a boiler room turned inside out
A baroque of plain plumbing not simplicity
Which is nothing he said
Rather a modest and secret complexity

The English sky wipes itself clean
And wind turbines thrash themselves
Like national champs in training

I put my arms around you and stop myself
Writing tales of backyard cargo cults
You nestle into the hollow of my dream
Which I want to write out but my eyes are full
Of rusty girders over soupy canals

You frown in your sleep that lulls the jargon
And crackle of newsprint with its fleet score
The trim roofs of shopping palaces steam
Over canopic jars full of carbonised laurel stalks

The painted masks bear no relation
Household gods composted with household goods

This is the poem that carries your dream
Or the city built of dream:
                                        two skyscrapers
Ride the wind like Twin Towers turned airliners
One buffets the other spitting dust it sparks it jolts
From its flight racked with strain it sinks like night

Dives into ocean there is no land there is no terror
Through the windows citizens wonder at frisking whale-sharks
The sealed half-city buoys to surface it soars up dripping
To swap this orbit with its twin in ritual collision and crash

This raw and impure music proves
That life is both beautiful and a struggle still

The dark girl with the big smile sings
In the Iraqi Restaurant on a level with the heavens
She unbolts a window and releases a dove

3 Out of the Way

The Netherlands

Brushing the dawn from her eyes there's somebody
Turning away in the mirror as she eases into her life
A dream of modest comfort as she turns into ours

Tacked to the mirror are postcards to make this home
A reflection of an elsewhere that has to be escaped

She is repeatedly passing through constantly
Almost outside and when the spaces are filled
There's no more room on her passport
She travels far to get it stamped each week

As she uncurls her lip unveils her long hair to face
The face that places the room's yellow restrictions
Sunlight slants across the bunk-bed like a slogan
A promise of belonging out of range of her longing
She curls her dark toes burrowed in synthetic fur

Afghanistan

Like a figure in a dream of perfect falling
Like something from somewhere like hell

You were the dark-eyed girl who crept out
Before the pink meat dawn to spy
The growling machines while the whole town
Still dreamt of exactly what she saw

Night vision green flecked with sparks
And clouds of vectoral vapour pouring across
Sun-baked gravel where a human head severe
And severed scarved in crackling plastic
Resurrected. She dived through coils of barbed wire

She ran her oily fingers along the sealed walls
Of the outsiders as though reading their secret script
Or leaving her own

Lebanon

Bodies or body-parts sheathed in taut plastic
Are portered on men's shoulders lightly
One-handed. Free fists punch at the stink
That long dry eyelashes brush masked from

Fluidarity is not contamination but he's alone
In the stairwell one electric light throws his big
Shadow across the wall like a stain
Slouched in his vest and trackie-bottoms
He frowns at the radio the local news whistles

Ana Am Bihlam phases like a remix as he
Pinches the bridge of his nose from elsewhere
The Voice of Catastrophe coughs in his ear

Later he will salute his crumpled car his tumbled
Satellite dish on his rebellious tiptoe through rubble

Iran

Young women slice-eyed and bushy browed
Between scarf-line and mask stand guard
In neatly stitched green canvas suicide vests
Three panniers with girl-guide toggles secure
Over the trailing pitch of life-long widowhood

*

Young women blonde as the West and plucked
Flutter around each other's gloss and pucker
They imagine their other lips moistened mutual
Red-nailed fingertips stroking illicit passions out

*

Young women dance on the illegal
                                        satellite screen high-heeled
The family lifts its curly-headed cherub
                                                into their silhouettes

*

Young women shopping flirt with headscarf infringements
Laugh under the massive image attack its open-top promise
A long-haired hunk delivering the goods

London

The new twenty-pound note feels crisp as a fake
As Adam Smith lectures us on division
Over a Chelsea bun and a white plastic knife

Through the cafeteria window with its view of the car park
The sun's weak eye at dusk spies the legend
And white men on green signs follow its arrows.
Waiting in the disabled bay between the Nissans

Beneath the limp Swedish flag the lank Union Jack
The Hindu family in pink and salmon grins

We're unstable before this excitation of price tags
A heady Sale as goods levitate before us
We surrender a pony to a dark-eyed migrant labourer
Despite our poor kind speech she gathers none of it
The white disk sinks below the pyramid of returns

Liverpool: 2 July 2007

Blue and white tape dips across the mouth
Of Ramilies Road and rattles in the gusts
Where a film crew preens its microphone fur
And jokes with a lone policeman who kicks the kerb

A smart car hops the speed bumps like a sparrow
The newspaper I clutch tells of 'fingertip searches'

The invisible man with the telephoto lens
Cranes its neck at the distant yellow jackets
Ambling between the police vans
This is almost as ordinary as the rain
Under the railway bridge I shelter from it

A downpour and its rebound on tarmac
So thick it fluffs up an ankle-deep fur
My soaked local paper brings the global home

4 Out of Nowhere

You build from song
an architecture of tumbles

a dance of stumbles on a shelf of air.
You name this the space left by the human.
You excavate Babylon or the strata of resting Jews
and the ribbons of tight ink on Pinkas Synagogue wall
with the surnames' bejewelled rubrication

(Whenever erased they're re-written
the act of their scrubbing
inscribed anew)

Stones leaning splinter through time
for those with no names
possess no death. You ex-
hume the ex-human in human unfinish

for Stephen

The red metronome on Letná hill
sways like a lucky drunkard
on its pedestal above the spires
a restless reminder of rust and wreck.
Or an antique windscreen wiper

describing its arc
upon a plane of smear and rain-wash
heroic in a monochrome movie, tinted red

With each wipe across the screen
the determined visage of the driver clears.
It's Josef Stalin the giant blocks with his pocks
long blown to shatters but he's still there

waving yes and no
to anyone who can see him

After the Last Word
of the dead text necrophiles come
our next words
which yet survive

as reasons
for living happily out
of nowhere and now

and then on to multitopia bearing
the stories so far

whose passions read as co-
eval becomings
geographies of affect in
capital Isness where
human unfinish is all about

'. . . comme l'aube l'azur timide . . .'

She hangs heavy from her corset for this story
so far. She raises the arc of one red-dotted brow
and flutters firework lashes at her fist-headed vamp

They scowl into each other's dark eyes but see only
nipples espying their true love through peepholes

The boy loves their leather fronds their clamped chokers.
He licks along twisted seams across buckled tattoos
through the purple mesh on their big legs swinging.
They mould themselves with man-maid passions.
She pushes her sex through his clench of meat

until her blind phallus drops as its straps sag.
Chained cuffs cover his un-pouched cock-ring.
She shrinks his gaze she bites her fake nails
while her lover's glove kisses his lips, and he swoons

for Patricia

The young couples in the crushed Amsterdam bar
dance to Barry White in the old-fashioned way

Later, aloft on Belgian beer, I murmur that I
love you, but then slip away, like the dancers,
into the night, knocking over bicycles chained
to bollards, and singing; into my reverie so far
in which we sit again drinking under the wooden ape

Almost human it grins at us both with more teeth
than the accordion it fumbles. This is all times
becoming a new time which is a now time
becoming all, a swoon through cracks in the paving

where vanished children crouch over hidden play.
Next day, a narrow canal house lips at its reflection;
we stand in front of it to stand for ourselves

The poem sends itself from anywhere
to your little box there it replays it
over and over. No redial no recall.
Dead ears drop in your lap. Pause.
No reply possible skip onto Message Two

I see the twin cathedrals they're twisting below
terror has been hijacked by artifice. Commas cower
along Hope St as we torque above them out of control
spluttering towards the radio tower full stop

That was your fake captain speaking
through me printing fear backwards
through his script. Out of nowhere

You receive my wild meanings
and divine unfinish in his spliced last word

April–August 2007

Byron James is Okay

for Allen Fisher

Text phone no-name news-clips
Shatter the showered details. *If*
Was *when*ed in the burnished air, a tin-
Can chrysalis *formerly* a double-decker bus.

Only the city has a name. It's calm.
Fluttery police tapes. Shivering faces
Covered with soot. Lacerations of sand-
Grain particles. Who walked over bodies; others,

Dismembered, still in their seats. Anon-
Ymous heroes beside pockmarked walls patch up
No bodies 'burning in fear'—above shaky sounds

Of movement under ground. Police fumble with a
Geodesic tent funnelled to the mouth of the Tube.
They call the unnamed names back to the world.

8 July 2005

Notes

This work—four sets of 24 sonnet forms plus four poems, making 100—is highly allusive to the language of the 'war on terror' waged after September 11 2001. Too many phrases filled the air for me to annotate them. However, there is a sense of indebtedness and thanks in the borrowings, transformations and cross-references listed below.

The title 'The War had ended, it had not Ended' is the last line of a poem by Denise Levertov, 'In California During the Gulf War', printed on the back cover of *The Poker* 2, Spring 2003. These poems themselves form a link with my project *Twentieth Century Blues*, by extending the 'Killing Boxes' strand beyond the original 7, which were concerned with the first Gulf War.

The prose piece 'Closing the Books: Locking the Chests' in *Hymns to the God in which my Typewriter Believes*, Exeter: Stride, 2006, may be considered another precursor. The works' initial poetics were displayed in 'Rattling the Bones (for Adrian Clarke)', which may be read on the *Softblow* webzine (www.softblow.com).

In the poem 'Dissensus-uncensored citizens...' in 'September 12', the term 'dissensus' is taken from Félix Guattari's late essay *The Three Ecologies*, London and New Brunswick: The Athlone Press, 2000. That same poem quotes Adorno.

'Smoking Gun' was written with the help of the compendious photo image-hoard collected and collated by Hans-Peter Feldmann in his *Voyeur* (Köln: Verlag der Buchhandlung Walther König, 1997).

In 'Ordinary Renditions', 'Toussaint' in 'Not just that all objects . . .' is the New Orleans musician Allen Toussaint.

In 'Warrant Error', there are embedded quotations from Hannah Arendt, Jorge Luis Borges, Gilles Deleuze, Jacques Derrida, Terry Eagleton, Doreen Massey, Peter Riley quoting

Francis Ponge, and Philip Roth, particularly in part four, 'Out of Nowhere', but also in dispersed form in part one, 'Off the Books', which also quotes and distorts numerous other voices. In 'English Sonnets' the voice of Nabeel Hussain, a victim of warrant error, survives relatively undistorted. 'Out of the Way' owes to the photographers Marieke van der Velden. Rodriho Abd, Stepanie Sinclair, Newsha Tavakolian and Tom Craig, featured in the exhibition *Risk* (Foam_Fotografiemuseum, Amsterdam, 2006), published in *Risk*, World Press Photo Joop Swart Masterclass 2006 (Amsterdam: World Press Photo, 2006), although the final poem's visual data I saw with my own eyes. In the poem 'Lebanon', 'Ana Am Bihlam' means 'I am dreaming', and is the title of a 1995 Lebanese pop song by Majida El Roumi, and may be heard on CD1 ('Arabian Classics') of *Beginner's Guide to Arabia*, Nacente Records. In 'Out of Nowhere', 'The Space Left by the Human' is the title of an art work by Adriena Šimotová in Prague City Art Gallery (c. 1986), and 'Excavate Babylon' quotes Kafka from a café wall in Prague. Pinkas Synagogue and Letná Hill are also both in Prague. The epigraph to 'She hangs heavy . . .' comes from Verlaine's poem 'Printemps' from *Parallèlement* (1889).

The title 'Byron James is Okay' was drawn from a text message sent to Sky News on the morning of 7 July 2005. The wonders of Google meant that within days of the poem partially appearing on Paul A. Green's website, Mr James and I were in email contact, and exchanging information. In particular I learnt of his movements on that day. There is something emblematic (and optimistic) about our brief exchange in relation to the poem's last line.

Robert Sheppard
7 July 2008

ACKNOWLEDGEMENTS

Some of these poems have appeared in the following anthologies: ed. Todd Swift, *Poems for Lord Hutton*. London: nthposition, 2003, www.nthposition.com; ed. Todd Swift, *Babylon Burning: 9/11 five years on*. London: nthposition, 2006, www.nthposition.com/babylonburning911.php; ed. Alan Corkish, *Liverpool Poets 08*. Liverpool: erbacce-press, 2008; ed. Jeff Hilson, *The Reality Street Book of Sonnets*. Hastings: Reality Street Editions, 2008, and ed. Patricia Scanlan, *Uplift: A Samizdat for Lee Harwood from his Friends*. Portslade: Artery Editions, 2008.

Some of these poems, or their earlier versions, have appeared in the following magazines: *English, Intercapillary Space, Jacket, New Writing, Pages, Parameter, Poetry Salzburg Review, Shadowtrain, Shearsman, Skald, Stimulus→Respond, Stride.*

Eight poems from 'September 12' appear on the audio CD *Points of Reference, Edge Hill University Poets*, Edge Hill University, 2007. Parts of the project may be heard on the online at Archive of the Now (www.archiveofthenow.com). Some poems were read on Rob Holloway's 'Up for Air', Resonance FM, 5 November 2003.

'Byron James is Okay' first appeared in *The Poetry Buzz*, a book for Allen Fisher's birthday perambulations around post 21/7 London on 23 July 2005, although part of it also appeared on Paul A. Green's website.

Poems from this book have been read at a number of poetry venues in Britain (and in Berlin in November 2007) and the entire sequence was read at the long-poem reading at Furzedown, Dartmoor, organised by philip kuhn, in September 2007.

Thanks to all the dedicated editors and poetry activists involved.

The author would like to gratefully acknowledge receipt of funding from the Edge Hill University Research Development Fund in the writing of this book.

www.ingramcontent.com/pod-product-compliance
Lightning Source LLC
Chambersburg PA
CBHW031155160426
43193CB00008B/375
* 9 7 8 1 8 4 8 6 1 0 1 8 7 *